KITTY O'NEIL

Daredevil Woman

by KARIN IRELAND

Harvey House, Publishers
New York, New York

Copyright © 1980 by Karin Ireland

All rights reserved, including
the right to reproduce this book
or portions thereof in any form.

Manufactured in the United States of America
ISBN 0-8178-0004-2
Library of Congress Catalog Card No. 80-80604
Published in Canada by Fitzhenry & Whiteside, Ltd., Toronto

HARVEY HOUSE, Publishers
20 Waterside Plaza, New York, New York 10010

For Tom, with love

I would like to thank Andree Williams, Chuck Duncan and Tom Justice for all their time and enthusiasm.

And thanks also to my friend Elizabeth Van Steenwyk, who knows how much she helped.

Chapter One

There's a tiny figure way up on top of that hotel roof. The camera moves in. It's Wonder Woman. She comes closer to the edge, too close. It looks as if . . . she is . . . she's going to jump. She steps off the roof and drops like a rock through the air. Somehow she lands without a scratch and hurries off after the villain.

How did Lynda Carter *do* that, anyway? Actually, Lynda didn't. Stuntwoman Kitty O'Neil made the jump for her, 12 floors, from the top of the Sheraton Universal Hotel. That's 127 feet, straight down.

Stunting can be a dangerous business. Every move has to be very well planned. And Kitty, who is deaf, has to take extra precautions. But she is good at what she does, she is very well trained. And she loves the feeling of falling through the air. She has since she was a little girl.

When Kitty was four years old she discovered that

the old-fashioned laundry chute in her grandmother's huge four-story house where they lived made a wonderful slide. The chute was meant to carry dirty clothes to the basement laundry. It was a perfect size for her, too.

When she felt like an adventure, she'd make her way up the stairs to the attic, hoping her mother wouldn't notice. Her excitement grew as she crossed the attic floor, then raised the small door on the wall. Heart pounding with anticipation she climbed so she was sitting on the ledge. Then she pushed off.

She couldn't hear the small door close behind her but she could "feel" the bang. Then suddenly it was pitch-dark and scary, like in a haunted house. She held her breath as she dropped with a delicious lurch in her tummy through the spooky insides of the house. She would land with a thud on the basement floor.

The nails that caught at her dress didn't bother her. She scurried back up the stairs to do it again.

"Kitty," her mother would say that night as she helped her get ready for bed, "look at the tears in this dress. You've been up to your old stunts, sliding down the laundry chute again, haven't you?"

Then Patsy O'Neil would shake her head and sigh.

But wasn't that what she really wanted? Kitty was curious and daring. Lots of children start out that way but are made timid by worried parents. Mrs. O'Neil had been careful never to make Kitty afraid to try something. She would not give her reason to doubt her abilities. As a result, her daughter had tremendous confidence in herself. Wasn't that confidence what was going to help Kitty lead a normal life?

Kitty, age nine.

When Kitty was only four months old she was terribly ill. Somehow she came down with measles, mumps, and smallpox, all at the same time. To be that sick at any age is dangerous. For a tiny baby it's even worse. She cried and shook her tiny feet and fists angrily while her mother tried everything she knew to make her more comfortable. Then Kitty's temperature soared and she lay too sick to be angry, too sick even to whimper.

For four days she lay still, her little body burning. Her mother was desperate. Kitty was going to die! Wasn't there *anything* she could do? A doctor might be able to help, she thought, but there weren't any around. They were all all taking care of the soldiers in World War II.

Finally a friend who was a nurse came to help. She took one look at Kitty and ordered her packed in ice, not sure they weren't already too late, but even as a baby Kitty could handle a challenge. Maybe being half-Cherokee and half-Irish helped. She fought back and got well.

But even as a baby Kitty could handle a challenge. Maybe being half Cherokee and half Irish helped. She fought back and got well.

A few months later, her father John O'Neil II got out of the Air Forece. He went into the oil and cattle business and the family moved into his mother's huge house.

The next year another baby, John O'Neill III, was

born. Kitty's parents were busy with him and it was a while before they realized how often she ignored their calls to her. When they did, they thought she was just being stubborn. Or maybe she was just jealous because the new baby took so much of their time.

Slowly they noticed there were other things she wasn't responding to, too. Baby John cried, startled, when wind blew a door closed with a bang. Kitty went right on playing with her blocks. She didn't even seem to notice.

Then Kitty was two, and though she was making a lot of sounds, none of them were words yet. Her parents began to watch her carefully. They began to realize how much she missed of what was going on right behind her back. They more they watched, the more worried they became.

They took her to a doctor who examined her and who told them what they feared was true. Her ears had been badly damaged when she was sick. Their two-year-old daughter was deaf. They sat in his office, stunned. It was frightening to suspect it between themselves, but to have it confirmed was a crushing blow. They had prayed to be told they were wrong.

The family had money and would do anything to help her hear, but all the money in Texas couldn't repair the damage the virus had done.

After they had gotten over the shock, her parents determined Kitty would not grow up to be different. Many deaf people are protected and isolated from the rest of the world because they can't understand what is being said. If they learn hand sign they can communicate with others who also know hand sign. But that's all! Many deaf people never learn how to talk. Kitty's parents vowed that she would learn to talk, and to talk well. But how could she learn to talk when she couldn't hear the words?

They spent weeks searching for every bit of information about deaf education they could find. Then they decided the answer was the John Tracy Clinic in California. Instructors there had taught thousands of people how to teach deaf children to talk and read lips. Kitty and her mother traveled west.

Back home in Texas, they started the training that would take most of their days and nights for the next six years. Hundreds of times a day Mrs. O'Neil would wave her arms to catch her daughter's attention. Kitty would come and sit facing her mother.

"Papa," said Mrs. O'Neil, and pointed to Kitty's father.
"Papa," she said again, holding Kitty's hand against her own throat so the little girl could feel the vibrations.
"Papa," she said a third time, holding Kitty's open palm in front of her own lips so Kitty could feel the air escaping her mother's mouth.

"Mama," her mother said then, going through the series again. After that, something else would be pointed to and named. And after that, something else, over and over again. Kitty usually enjoyed the attention, even though she didn't know what it was all about.

Often, though, while they worked she would suddenly spot a toy lying on the floor and want to stop working and play. Or John would charge through the room and she would long to follow him. Mrs. O'Neil would have to shake her head and say no. There would be a little time to play with John later, but now Kitty had to learn to talk.

Lessons continued with everything being named while her mother shopped or cooked or cleaned house. Kitty chattered away happily too, but none of her sounds came even close to the ones her mother made. Kitty chattered while pretending to cook. She copied her mother's house cleaning, too. Then one day when she was almost three she copied something new.

"Mama," said Mrs. O'Neil patiently pointing to herself for the ten-thousandth time.

"Mama," she said again with Kitty's hand at her throat.

"Mama!" said Kitty pointing at her mother. "Mama!" Kitty saw her mother's eyes fly open with surprise, then suddenly fill with tears. Then a huge smile covered her face. Suddenly she was swept up and waltzed around the room held tight in her mother's arms. She knew she had done something very right!

It was a big, big step for her to say her first word, but it was the result of long months of trial and error. Each new word would take just as much work to learn. The all-day-every-day lessons continued.

Mrs. O'Neil found there were other deaf children in Wichita Falls, Texas, and other mothers who wanted them to learn to talk. They found an old house to rent and opened the School of Listening Eyes. Mrs. O'Neil was the school's first teacher, sharing what she had learned at the John Tracy Clinic.

Moving her lessons from home to the school was fun for Kitty. There were twenty other deaf children there with her and she thought it great fun to have so many new friends.

Mrs. O'Neil made the children work very hard. Each child had to learn each word in the same tedious way Kitty had been learning at home. But there was time for fun things there too, like parties, and lessons with the dance teacher who came to teach them ballet and tap.

Kitty watched the teacher and was quick to copy the moves she made. She loved to dance, and followed the beat of the music easily as the vibrations drummed gently against her skin.

Sometimes everybody took the afternoon off to go swimming. Kitty was four the first time she saw somebody jump from a diving board. Right away she knew she had to do it too. She ran to where her mother sat beside the pool.

"I want to do that," she said, pointing excitedly at the board.

"But Kitty, you don't know how to swim," her mother said.

"I want do do it," she insisted eagerly.

Mrs. O'Neil asked the lifeguard to go to the deep end to catch her daughter. Kitty climbed up on the board and walked to the end and jumped! When she came up there was a great big smile on her face. That was fun! She hurried to do it again.

As her mother watched she decided it was time for swimming lessons. Kitty's dad started teaching her at home. Kitty felt very close to her father and looked forward to the lessons with him. She caught on fast and was swimming well in no time, but her favorite way to cross the pool was still on her daddy's back.

When he was home she tagged along after him whenever she could. One lazy summer day Kitty sat on the porch watching him mow the lawn with a power mower. Even from across the yard the vibrations tickled against her skin. She liked the feeling. She ran over and shouted at him.

Kitty diving in competition in Wichita Falls, Texas, age fifteen.

"Daddy, may I ride on the mower?"

"No," he answered, "you have a dress on and it's dangerous."

Kitty ran into the house and her dad went back to mowing. Then the front door banged and Kitty came out in a shirt and pants.

"*Now* can I ride?" she asked. Her father smiled but shook his head and still said no, it's dangerous. But Kitty was so disappointed she started to cry. Her father gave in and perched her on top of the mower. She got her ride. And what an exciting ride it was! The vibrations were so much stronger when she was actually touching the mower.

Kitty continued to be a good student at the School of Listening Eyes, picking up new words slowly, one at a time.

One morning when she was six she woke up ready to go to school and was surprised to see her mother had set out a Sunday dress.

"We're going to Houston," said Mrs. O'Neil, "to have you fitted for a hearing aid." Kitty didn't know what that was, but her mother's enthusiasm rubbed off on her. She was always ready for an adventure.

Chapter Two

Kitty and her mother sat in a little room while a doctor took a hearing aid out of a drawer. "Your daughter won't be able to hear much," he explained to Mrs. O'Neil. "Her ears are badly damaged. But maybe she will be able to pick up some sounds around her."

Kitty watched as he brough the contraption to her and fitted a plug in each ear. "There you go, Kitty," she saw him say. He flicked a small switch.

Suddenly a painful whistling sound tore at her ears and seemed to split her head in two. It was terrible! And it hurt! She ripped the plugs out and covered her ears with her hands. No way was she going to wear that whistling monster! No way!

The doctor made some adjustments and got Kitty to give it another try. Hearing aids were not very good in those days. It still hurt and she wouldn't wear it. She just didn't see any reason why she should.

Her mother thanked the doctor and took the hearing aid home anyway, thinking somehow she'd get Kitty to use it.

But she never did. Kitty had another objection besides the noise it made. These days she had more time away from her lessons. She liked to swim and play baseball and football with her brother and his friends. How could she be active in sports with those wires coming out of her head and that *thing* hanging there on her chest?

By the time Kitty was eight she was good at beginning arithmetic and she could read lips well. Her mother took her out of the School of Listening Eyes and sent her to Chickisha, Oklahoma, to spend a year at the Jane Brooks School for the Deaf. She lived there in a dorm with other deaf children and that year she learned to read and write.

When she came home for summer vacation her mother said she would be going to public school in September. Kitty was excited about that. She still didn't realize most of the children she knew were deaf, and that being deaf was different than being able to hear. She didn't realize she'd be moving into another world.

She only knew she'd be going to the same school as her brother.

The school bell rang that first day and all the children found a place to sit. Then her excitement was quickly crushed. "Kitty," the teacher said, "*you* come sit up here in the front row." Kitty got up, wondering why she was the only one that had to change her seat. If the other kids could read lips from the back row why wouldn't the teacher let her?

As the day went on she noticed some of the children making fun of the way she talked. She noticed other things that began to make her feel lonely and sad. As the hours passed she realized that somehow she was different from the other children.

After school she ran home close to tears. She took the porch steps two at a time and let the door close behind her with a bang.

Mrs. O'Neil looked quickly at her daughter then set down the blouse she was mending. Mr. O'Neil changed his mind about going upstairs and sat down on the nearest chair.

Kitty let all the questions of the morning tumble out. Whey did those kids talk so much more than she did? And how could they do it without even looking at each other? How could kids on one side of the room answer questions the teacher had asked facing the other? They couldn't possibly have seen her lips! And why did the kids laugh when she answered the teacher's questions? She knew she had answered them right. Why was she so different from them?

"You are deaf," her mother said simply, "they can hear. Just don't worry about them."
"Kitty, do your school work," her father added, "and get involved in sports."

Her parents knew they were asking a lot. But they couldn't let Kitty feel sorry for herself. They knew she was a terrific little girl, bright and athletic, and she had a wonderful sense of humor. These were the important things, not that she couldn't hear. She'd never be strong and independent if she felt sorry for herself.

Kitty took her parents' advice, trying to pay attention to the teacher and ignore the children's taunts and jeers. At home she finished her homework before letting herself go find her brother. At school she threw herself into whatever sports were played. She didn't let it show that it hurt to be chosen last on someone's team.

After a while the kids decided it wasn't that much fun to tease someone who wouldn't react. When they got to know her they discovered she was really nice and was fun to be with, and she was better at sports than most of them. Then it was always a scramble to see who could have Kitty on their team.

She played after school every chance she got, too. She got scrapes, bruises, and sometimes black eyes playing baseball and football with her brother and his friends. Sometimes their teasing led to fist fights, but her brother had taught her how to protect herself and Kitty remembers winning most of the time. Her parents didn't interfere.

Her mother had a unique way to tempt Kitty to do even more. Whenever she or John asked for money to go to the movies Mrs. O'Neil made them work for it.

"Swim 40 laps of the pool," she'd say, "and you can have a dollar." There was an old mud hole near home, about ten feet deep, and at the edge stood an old tower. Sometimes Mrs. O'Neil would say, "whoever jumps into the water from highest up the tower can have a dollar," and the kids would race each other to the pond.

Once when John jumped he got stuck underwater in the mud at the bottom. When he didn't come up, Kitty jumped in to try to help. She pulled and he struggled and finally got loose in time. Neither of them thought much about how dangerous that could have been — they were in too much of a hurry to get back to claim the money.

Away from home, Kitty jumped from motel balconies into swimming pools. Luckily she never missed. She wasn't so lucky the day she challenged John to a bicycle race down a hill near her grandmother's house.

"Bet I can beat you to the bottom," she said. They were always competing with each other, so of course John said, "You're on!"

Ready, go! They were off. Kitty enjoyed that familiar thrill of speed as she flew down the steep hill. The wind whipped at her hair and rushed against her face. It was terrific. Then her front tire hit a rock and she lost control. The bike bounced, then swerved at a crazy

Kitty with her brother John III when Kitty was seventeen.

angle for what seemed like forever. Then she fell, scraping her way down the hill on one bare arm. Tiny rocks ripped off the skin and clung to the blood. That was one race John won.

When Kitty was in fifth grade an ice skating show came to town and she and her mother went. As she watched the skaters fly across the ice she knew she had to learn too. As usual, her parents encouraged her to get involved. She loved the hours she spent flashing across the ice, crisp air tingling at her face. She loved the speed. For a while she went skating every day, then it was no longer a challenge and she wanted to try something new.

There was a piano in the house. She decided to learn to play that and was quick to catch on. She could feel the vibrations the notes made, she could "feel it" when she hit the wrong note. She learned to play the cello too by feeling the vibrations and learning to recognize which ones were right.

She was so busy with her own life she hardly noticed how much her parents had begun to argue. It came as a shock to her when they decided to divorce. She and her father kept in close touch when he moved, and secretly she hoped her parents would soon get back together.

Then one day that dream was shattered forever as she got the terrible news. Her father had been flying a small plane in the mountains. He had got caught in a downdraft while taking off and hadn't been able to pull the plane up. He had crashed and died. It was a terrible, aching blow. What would she ever do without him?

Chapter Three

Kitty took her father's death hard. There had been a strong bond between them that living in separate houses couldn't change. But now . . . She would never, ever see him again. She would never feel his strong hand in hers or see his teasing smile. The hurt made nothing else seem like fun.

After a few weeks, Mrs. O'Neil told Kitty and John they were going to move. Kitty started helping her mother clean up and pack. While emptying out a closet she found a scrapbook of her father's that she had never known he had. As she opened the book fresh tears and floods of memories came to her. He had always been so good to her, always encouraging her, always giving her support. What had she ever given him?

Leafing sadly through the pages she was surprised to discover he had been a competitive swimmer when he was young. She remembered their lessons in the pool. She still liked to swim, but until that moment had never thought of swimming on a team. But her dad had done it, and suddenly she wanted to more than anything in the world.

She closed the scrapbook and told herself she would become a *good* swimmer. She would work hard. She would work harder at everything else she did too. She felt sure her dad was watching her from Heaven. She would make him proud of her.

Kitty joined the local YWCA swim team, the Mermaids. The laps she had swum at home to make money to go to the movies made her a natural 100-meter sprinter. All her life she had competed with her brother. Here were some new people to compete with, and Kitty liked the challenge. These girls accepted her at once. Here, what you could do in the pool was what was important, and Kitty did well. She could swim fast and, even though she couldn't hear, she could *feel* the concussion of the starting gun. Because she was not distracted by other sounds, she often hit the water first.

She loved it when she won an event. Her teammates loved it too. Kitty thought they were the only ones who cared. One day there was a large meet and she won *three* events. The next morning she got a surprise.

"Look at this, Kitty," her mother said, handing her the paper. She looked and there was her name, with a story about her wins. She read it with a new understanding. It wasn't just important to her and the team. Other people who weren't even swimmers cared about it too. She decided to work even harder. During the summer she practiced eight hours a day. In the winter she practiced after school in the Y's indoor pool.

Even with her busy schedule, she and her brother stayed close. He took her hunting and taught her how to use a shotgun. He took her fishing, too. Sometimes he'd come home with a frog and she'd scream at him. Not because she minded the frog, but because he brought it home to cook and eat!

Kitty continued to swim and in the following years she won at dozens of other meets. One swim practice session when she was 14 started out like all the others, but it made a big change in her life. The team was getting ready to compete in a big meet in Oklahoma. Word came that one of the divers was sick and would not be able to go. The coach looked disappointed at the news.

"I'll do it," Kitty said excitedly. "I'll do it, I'll dive."

The coach frowned and shook his head. "No," he said, "you're a swimmer, not a diver. You've never done it before."

"I can do it," she insisted, "I'll show you I can." She hurried to the board and let a dive she'd seen someone else do play in her mind. Then she stepped forward and dived.

When she came up, the mixed look of surprise and excitement on the coach's face told her she would be diving in the meet.

In Oklahoma the stadium was filled with spectators. It was time for the meet to begin. Kitty stood with her teammates and looked at the rows of faces watching the pool. It was exciting to know soon they would all be watching her.

She had been told what she would have to do and had practiced back at the Y. She watched the others dive. Then finally it was her turn. That old familiar feeling, the urge to tackle a challenge was strong as she climbed onto the board. She stood there a moment, blocking out everything but this board and the pool below. She ignored the butterflies of excitement that fluttered inside. She thought only about how she would do the dive, going through each move in her mind. Then she was ready. As she hit the water with a clean slice, she knew it had been good. It had been fun, too.

After all the dives had been completed, she felt an excitement that she had begun to miss with swimming. Then her name was called over the loud-speakers. She had not only had fun, but had won a third place trophy too. As Kitty went to accept her trophy she knew she had finished her swimming career. Now she wanted to become a diver.

She dove with the team for the next two years, adding more trophies, ribbons and medals to her collection.

When Kitty was 16 her mother saw her dive in a meet and was impressed. Kitty was really good. She could be even better, her mother thought, with the right coach. She asked around and learned that Dr. Sammy Lee, a two-time Olympic diving champion, was running a school in Anaheim, California for Olympic hopefuls. She decided Kitty should train with him. She packed their bags and without warning presented her daughter to the surprised coach.

Usually people wrote first, or called for an appointment, but Dr. Lee agreed to a tryout and was impressed with Kitty's skills. "You have a good chance to go to the 1964 Olympics in Tokyo," he said, after watching her dive. "Are you willing to work hard?" Kitty said she was and he accepted her as a student.

Mrs. O'Neil was still teaching at the School of Listening Eyes. She had to return to the school and to John III, who had stayed behind. It was arranged that for the first few months Kitty could stay with a family Dr. Lee knew.

Later, in a show of the independence her parents had tried to encourage, she got an apartment. At 16 she was on her own.

She enrolled in Savannah High School in Anaheim with her usual enthusiasm, but she was quickly disappointed. In Texas she had gone to a private girls' school. Everyone knew her and she had had lots of friends, but there were boys at Savannah and somehow that made the girls different, harder to get to know. They were too busy trying to impress the boys to take time to get to know this quiet newcomer.

There were times when she longed for her friends in Texas, friends who cared about things she cared about and didn't laugh at the way she talked. Then she'd tell herself it didn't matter. She'd show everyone deaf people are just like anybody else. She'd become a championship diver. That would stop them from laughing at her.

Mornings she spent in school. Then after a quick lunch she went to spend every afternoon practicing three-meter springboard and ten-meter platform dives with Dr. Lee.

Over and over and over she climbed up to practice the same dives, time after time after time. Dr. Lee cued his other students when to come out of tucks and twists by shouting; with Kitty he had to use a gun loaded with blanks.

He worked her harder than she had ever been worked before — he used a lot of blanks — but the practicing was paying off, she was getting better and better. Things were looking very good for Kitty. Then during a visit back to Texas she got involved in another life and death struggle.

She got sick, very sick. She had a high fever, and flashed from burning hot to cold. She vomited all the time and had terrible headaches. She was rushed to the hospital with spinal meningitis. There she got even sicker and was barely able to move.

Mrs. O'Neil tried to be positive. When Kitty had been so sick as a baby she had lived. This time there were plenty of doctors to help. She knew spinal meningitis could be fatal but she prayed her daughter would live.

She stayed by Kitty's bed for a solid week, encouraging her to fight, and Kitty did begin to fight. The headaches and fever left but, as she started feeling a little better, she noticed something else that terrified her. There was one whole side of her she still couldn't move! She tried to push the fears away. Surely that was just because she was still sick. That would go away when she was well. Wouldn't it?

Finally the doctor came to give his report on the future. "You were a very sick girl, Kitty," he said. "This paralysis you have may not go away but you should consider yourself very lucky to be alive."

Racing against other members of the Toyota Celebrity team, Toyota Grand Prix, Watkin's Glen, New York, October, 1976.

Kitty stared at him in disbelief. "Lucky to be half-paralyzed," she said, "no way! I'm going to start walking!" And while he stood there, mouth open in surprise, she threw back the bed covers, got up and stumbled across the room. For the rest of her stay she had a terrible time with the nurses who wanted her to rest in bed. But she asked them over and over, how can you practice walking when you're lying down?

The paralysis finally left but Kitty practically had to start over with her diving. Her timing was off. Just a little, but it mattered. She was not as strong as she had been, and she got tired more quickly. She had to get her muscles back in shape. She practiced and practiced and practiced. In early 1964 she was strong enough to win the AAU Junior Olympics Diving Championship. And she was good enough to qualify to go to the tryouts for the Olympics. The Olympics — everything she had done for the last two years was so she could go to the Olympics.

With the tryouts just two months away she had another stroke of bad luck doing a practice dive. Thumbs have to be locked tight together to enter the water at 40 mph but Kitty's slipped and one hand flew up and hit her forehead. It didn't take a doctor to tell her she had a broken wrist.

She knew the cast would be off in time, but it was frustrating to miss weeks of practice.

Finally the time for the tryouts had come. She knew it would be the toughest competition of her life. Here were the best, trying to out-dive the best. There would be lots of losers since only the top three would get to go to Tokyo.

Kitty watched carefully as each girl did her dives. She concentrated hard, going through each move in her mind before doing her own dive. She knew she was diving well, but so was everyone else. When the final scores were announced in the ten-meter platform category, Kitty's name was called twelfth. She had done a good job but it hadn't been enough.

Over the years she had won 38 blue ribbons, 17 first-place trophies and 31 gold medals swimming and diving. That seemed like a lot to her, and a lot of doing the same thing over and over. The next Olympics weren't until 1968. Did she want to keep doing it another four years? No, she decided, she didn't. It was time to do something else.

Something new, something exciting — her eyes sparkled, wondering what this new thing would be.

Chapter Four

Kitty had always loved motors and speed. She had made friends with some boys in the neighborhood and they had often invited her to go on their motorcycles or boats. Usually she had been too busy to accept, but now she had finished high school and she had finished diving. She had some money from a fund left by her dad so she didn't have to work right away. She had time to get involved in their kind of sports.

The friend across the street with the boat took her deep-sea diving and taught her to water ski. The friend with the motorcycle taught her how to ride. It wasn't long before she had two motorcycles of her own and was racing them on weekends. Motors and speed — she had found her new thing to get involved in.

It wasn't long before another friend got her into racing cars. Sometimes she'd compete nearly every other week.

She bought a dune buggy and started racing it in desert events. She raced friend Ky Michaelson's rocket-powered snowmobile too, but not in competition. She did that just for fun.

Kitty enjoyed these friends who were as interested in sports as she was. She enjoyed having the time to do whatever she wanted without spending most of her day in the water. She didn't like water very much anymore. Actually things were just about perfect. Then in 1969 her mother had a stroke and died. Kitty was sad, but she was older than when her father had died. She knew she would miss her mother very much but she accepted her death as a part of life. In quiet times, as Kitty thought of the things she had done in her life, she remembered her mother and knew her mother's years of teaching had made it all possible.

Three years later she found out that her mother's school had been closed for lack of money. She was sad that no one had told her before, no one had given her a chance to try to keep it open. She silently promised her mother that one day she'd open her own deaf school.

In 1970 Kitty was water skiing so fast her friends talked her into trying for a speed record. The plan they worked out was for her to start off skiing like normal. The driver would then go faster and faster until Kitty gave the signal to stop or she fell. The spotter would relay what was happening with her to the driver of the boat. They all hoped she would signal first. A fall at the speeds they were thinking about could really hurt her badly.

They arranged for an official to be there to watch. They would make only one run. Kitty started off slow to get the feel of the water. The spotter sat facing the back of the boat watching her. She looked good and strong. Then the boat started to pick up speed. The engine roared, they went faster and faster. The speedometer needle hit 50, 60, 70, then 80, 90, it was over the 100 mph mark. Kitty was flashing across the water at over 100 mph. It was a record. Her official time was 104.85 mph!

Sometimes childhood memories drew her back to Texas but she always returned to California. It was her

After an hour of racing, reaching speeds up to 120 m.p.h., Kitty wins 4th place in the Celebrity Division, Toyota Grand Prix, October, 1976. Photo Credit: Joanna Miles.

Kitty with the Celebrity Team, Toyota Grand Prix, October, 1976.

home now. True, she had met people there who took advantage of her because she was so trusting, and that hurt, but she had a lot of good friends too. And it was a good place to be for sports.

She continued to race cars in off-road meets, competing against pros like Mickey Thompson, Bobby Ferro, Johnny Johnson, Gary Bagelich, and Parnelli Jones.

In between she still raced motorcycles in desert and motocross events like the Mint 400, Mexican 1,000, and Baja 5000. In 1976 she entered an 80-mile race across the burning Mojave Desert, not knowing it would open a whole new world to her.

It was hot. Hot and noisy, with 300 competitors revving their bikes. The noise didn't bother Kitty a bit. The line of racers were ready, watching the starter. The flag dropped, they were off, tires spitting sand at anyone behind.

Kitty got a good start, and smiled as the wind whipped against her body. Already some racers were falling behind. Kitty stayed right out near the front. As the hours passed more racers fell behind, some stopped completely with engine trouble. Kitty was tired; it seemed even hotter than before. Her body was weary from bumping along on the bike for so long. Still, it was fun, too. Up ahead were two guys she'd been watching, trying to catch for the last hour or so. They had been watching her too, and were determined not to be caught.

The race was an 80-mile sandy loop. They had gone 40 miles in one direction, turned, and come almost all the 40 miles back. Kitty saw the finish line ahead. She urged her bike to go faster, faster, and finished close on the tails of J.N. Roberts and Alan Gibbs.

Kitty after setting a new speedboat record of 285.23 m.p.h. at Walker Lake, Nevada, in 1977.

After the race Kitty walked over to them and asked, "Can I ride with you?"

They smiled and said, "Sure, if you can keep up."

"I did!" she reminded them, and they laughed and admitted she had.

After talking awhile they asked why her voice was so high-pitched and she told them it was because she was deaf. At first they didn't believe her. She did talk with a slight slur to some of her words but they thought it was some kind of an accent. She convinced them she was really deaf and they were even more impressed with her riding. It was surprising that this hundred-pound girl could handle her bike so well, but to do it without being able to hear which gear she was in was something else!

Kitty told them about her love of speed, and as they talked more she told them about her years as a diver.

"How would you like to be a stuntwoman?" they asked.

"What's that?" she asked.

They explained that actors and actresses usually aren't allowed to do scenes that might be dangerous, that stuntpeople do the scenes for them. They told her to go home and watch an action program on TV.

She looked at them doubtfully. "I don't know what to do," she said.

"Don't worry," they said, "we'll teach you."

She went home that night and watched stuntpeople fall and fight and crash cars in place of the actors in the story. That's what Alan and J.N. wanted her to learn to do, she realized. Strangely the idea didn't excite her very much, but she needed a job. It was time to start making money for her own deaf school. Stunting looked like something she could do. She decided to give it a try!

Chapter Five

J.N. and Alan arranged for her to be a part of a stunt show scheduled to raise money for the Braille Institute. Kitty arrived early to start her new career with no idea what they had in store for her.

"There's nothing to this gag," said Alan Gibbs casually, using the word they use for stunt. "Just go out and run around a while." Kitty watched as they zipped her into a heavy fireproof suit. Five minutes' worth of oxygen ran from a small tank, attached to her chest under her suit, through a tube to a mouthpiece which she clamped in her teeth. Just like scuba diving, she thought. Well, almost.

They put a helmet on her, closed the trap door and said, "Goodbye!" Then they set her on fire.

The chemical they had smeared on the suit flared at once. She was a human torch. It was hot inside the suit as she walked awkwardly around, waving her hands in the air. Then the men doused her with a fire extinguisher to put the flames out and peeled her out of the suit.

"That was a fire gag," Alan said.

"Oh," was all Kitty said. She was OK. But what a gag to do for the very first stunt!

Not long after that a producer at Universal Studios heard about her. He offered her a stunting job, a car roll. Could she do it? Kitty said yes, she could. He agreed to sponsor her into the Screen Actors Guild, and that was important to her. Without a sponsor she couldn't get the union card. Without the card she couldn't get a job in films.

She showed up early for her job, then waited. Finally they were ready for her and the director led her to the car. Kitty pulled on a helmet and settled down in the driver's seat. She fastened five harness seatbelts across her body one by one. These would hold her in place so she wouldn't get hurt bouncing around inside the car.

"Kitty," the director said, "just drive about 60 mph, hit the ramp, and you'll roll. OK?"

It was OK with her. She drove the route once slowly just for practice, then moved back into starting position. She looked up at the roof where a roll bar was built in to keep the roof from crushing down on her head. She remembered another safety precaution, a special tiny gas tank under the hood that held just enough gas for the stunt. That would help keep down the risk of fire.

Kitty cleared her mind of everything except the gag she was about to do. She went through each move carefully, just like she had done before diving. There. There was the wave signaling her to go ahead. The cameramen were ready for her.

She revved the motor and eased her foot off the brake. She was off. She was picking up speed, the ramp was coming closer, *now*. She hit it with her right tires, the car tipped. She slammed on the brakes and wrenched the steering wheel right. She was rolling. The car rattled and groaned as it slammed against the ground. The noise was so loud even she could hear some of it. Then the car settled back on its wheels. The shaking stopped, it was totally quiet again. People standing around applauded, the crew rushed over to make sure she was OK.

Kitty could "feel" it was a good roll. A lot safer, she thought, than the time she'd rolled her mom's Chevy in a Texas field. That was when she was only 16. Easier, too! In the field there hadn't been a ramp to help get the roll started.

Making it look real, Kitty fights off Tom Justice in preparation for a stunt.

She started getting calls to do other stunts. In between jobs she worked out with J.N. and Alan. She had a natural instinct for this kind of work but there was a lot she had to learn. They taught her how to fight, or how to make it look like she was fighting. They had her work on the trampoline practicing jumps and landings. When she got good on the trampoline they taught her how to fall into an air bag.

By practicing their stunts, Kitty and Tom are less likely to get hurt.

The producers for "Superstunt I" heard about her and asked her to do a gag in their show. She agreed. The script called for her to do a chase scene in a van, crash it, catch on fire, and jump from a roof. It was part of a little story that was making fun of TV detective shows. The van she drove was supposed to be carrying a girl who was kidnapped. The police were hot in pursuit.

Kitty raced down a busy boulevard. It was crowded — there were too many slow cars in her way. She was in a hurry, the police were catching up. She weaved in and out of lanes, missing other cars by what seemed to be just inches. She slid around corners with screaming tires then weaved in-and-out between more cars. The police were even closer now. She was in the middle lane. Suddenly she made a right turn. There was another car in the right lane! It swerved up onto the curb and Kitty made it past, aiming the van up a ramp and into a seven-story parking lot. The cops saw her, screeched through a turn, and followed her up the ramp. Up, up, and around they went. There was a wooden barrier at the top. She couldn't stop. She crashed through it and onto the roof of the parking lot. She made a sharp left, but there was a parked car right in her way. She hit it, the van rolled on its side, and exploded. Kitty climbed out. She was on fire! She ran to the edge of the roof and jumped seven floors straight down.

It was a spectacular stunt. It looked wild and daring, which is just the way it was supposed to look, but it had been carefully planned. The streets she drove on were closed off to normal traffic while she was there. Everyone driving was a professional and all the close calls were rehearsed at much slower speeds.

On the roof there was a ramp by the car that helped her tip the van. When it tipped there was a tiny fire under the van, then it went out and the camera stopped while Kitty climbed out and got into her fireproof suit. She climbed back in the van, it was set on fire, and the cameras were started again.

Kitty then climbed out, on fire, and made her way to the edge of the roof. Here the cameras stopped again. The crew put the fire out so she could concentrate on the next part, the jump. She looked down at the air bag, she blocked everything out, thinking only about the jump. She went through it once in her mind.

She waved her hand, signaling she was ready, and once more her suit was put on fire. The cameras started and she jumped, then landed in the air bag with a plop, still on fire.

As she hit, her body pushed the middle of the air bag down and the sides billowed up around her, covering her. The ground crew scrambled up on the bag, aiming fire extinguishers where they thought she was. She climbed out, smiling for the cameras. Later she told the crew she had been burned a little around her eyes, more proof of what she already knew was true — no gag is ever a completely safe one. Something can always go wrong.

Chapter Six

Kitty had been successful in almost everything she ever tried. Would she be able to make it in stunting too? People *were* calling her for jobs. Would they call her back for more?

It had been so easy for her to get her first job she was surprised to learn that hundreds of people come to Hollywood each year to be stuntpeople and usually only two or three make it. She had been lucky to get in. Would she be good enough to stay in?

She didn't have to wait long to find out. Directors were happy with her and they did call her back. She had that rare combination of daring backed by skill that is essential for a stuntperson. She was fun to work with, too. She was pleasant and cooperative, and had a great sense of humor. Everyone just felt good when they were with her. After only three months in the business, Kitty was one of the most called-for stuntwomen in Hollywood.

She wasn't just popular with directors. Other stuntpeople noticed how good she was too. One group of stuntmen was so impressed with her they considered her for membership in their all-male group. At a meeting on September 13, 1976 a vote was taken. The 37 men of Stunts Unlimited voted unanimously to accept her as a member.

Every day she got stacks of fan mail. The letters meant a lot to her. She felt that everyone who knew about her would realize that people don't have to be limited because they are deaf. She tried to find time to answer them herself.

She also got invitations from all over the United States to talk to children in schools for the deaf. She accepted them eagerly. Talking to these children was a special joy.

Soon so many job offers came in she had to start wearing a paging device fastened at her waist so she wouldn't miss any of them. Then when directors wanted her on short notice, they could call her answering service and leave a message there. An operator at the answering service would call another number that made Kitty's beeper vibrate. Kitty would feel it and know someone was trying to get in touch with her.

It was early morning, one of those rare Los Angeles summer days without smog. Kitty was just finishing her daily seven-mile run when her beeper went off. Someone was trying to reach her. Whom could she ask to phone the answering service to see what the call was about? She turned the tiny box off and headed to her car. Maybe her friend Chuck Duncan would be home. That was the only thing that bothered her about being deaf — she couldn't make her own phone calls.

She found Chuck and he called the answering service for the message. John at Universal Studios had called. Chuck dialed John's number. He listened, then turned to Kitty.

"John wants to know if you can do a gag at 11:00 this morning," he said.
"Today?" she asked.
"Yeah," answered Chuck.

She looked around for a clock, then nodded. Chuck talked again into the phone and hung up.

"OK, Kitty," he said. "Gate 14, 11:00." She didn't ask what the gag was. She knew John hadn't said. Unless it's something really big, stuntpeople usually aren't told much about a job until they're on the set. It could be almost anything.

Once she drove a new Lincoln in a demolition derby for TV's San Pedro Bums. Another time she raced a motorcycle around inside a house, finally falling in the living room, in the movie *Serial*.

She's done "near misses" with cars, being both the driver and the victim of this gag. Near misses are just what they sound like they are, gags where two or more of something *almost* hit. If she is the victim she may be crossing the street when a car runs a red light and comes at her, stopping at just the last moment. Or maybe the script calls for the car not to stop. Then she must wait until the last minute to jump out of the way.

Kitty wins first place in a charity donkey race for handicapped children.

She's also been "hit" when the script calls for it. In that gag a car might come at her and, instead of her getting out of the way, she must look as though she has been hit. What she does is wait until the very last minute, then *jump* up on the hood of the car, do a shoulder roll acaross the top, and roll off the other side. Timing has to be just right for this. If she waits too long, she can get badly hurt.

She slipped off a roof, grabbed at the ledge and hung by her fingers on TV's *Baretta*, and jumped 110 feet from the World Trade Center Building on *Eischied*.

In *Family* she crashed a car over a curb and into a telephone pole for Kristy McNichol, and she did a wild car chase through the streets of Los Angeles on a TV show, *Just Us Kids*. What was the chase like? She can't remember. She's driven so many fast cars so many places there was nothing special that stands out in her mind about that one.

What if she got on the set and the director outlined a stunt she didn't really want to do? It happens sometimes, she says, but if you're a stuntwoman you have to do the stunt. Some stuntpeople disagree but Kitty's attitude reflects her childhood. She learned to talk and swim and dive by doing what had to be done — like it or not. She carries that discipline into her work.

One stunt she didn't like was in *Airport '77* in which she had to drown for Lee Grant. The plane was supposed to have crashed in the ocean, and Kitty had to be swept through the plane.

Kitty stood in the aisle, then on cue hundreds of gallons of icy-cold water flooded the plane. Even though she knew it was coming, the giant wall of water hit her with a shock. It was cold! It was so powerful! She was instantly thrown off her feet and swept through the plane. Sometimes she was underneath, sometimes she managed to push her head up for a breath of air. Gasping and choking for real, she grabbed at seat backs and doorways not having to pretend too hard that her life was at stake. Later she hung face-down in the water for what seemed like forever while the cameras filmed her "drowned."

When the filming was finished Kitty went home, sick. The water had been too cold and she had been in it too long. It was hours before she could stop shaking from the cold.

Some stunts look OK beforehand, she just doesn't like the way they end. She did a fight scene on one show in which she was supposed to land on her bottom but landed on her head instead. Just part of her job, she says, but she saw stars on that one.

Then there was the jump she made on the *Mike Douglas Show*. She was to run across the stage and jump and land in the middle of the air bag. Mike turned in his chair to watch, Kitty ran, jumped and missed! Instead she landed on the back of her head on the hard floor.

Mike jumped to his feet and ran to help her up. "Kitty, are you OK?" he asked worriedly. "Here, do you want to sit down?"

"No," she answered, rubbing the back of her head. "I'm OK." She walked back across the stage and made the jump again. That time she landed right.

Her *Wonder Woman* jump was a different type. For it she jumped straight down. Luckily it went off perfectly. If she had missed the bag at 127 feet she would not have been able to get up and walk away.

She spent three days getting ready mentally for that *Wonder Woman* jump. That day she jumped two times from lower heights first, to test the feel of the air bag. If it were too full, she could bounce right off. She checked to see that she was landing in the middle of the bag. If she jumped out an inch too far, she could be off by several feet when she landed. She could be off by even more if she made the same error higher up.

As a double for Wonder Woman, Kitty jumps 127 feet from the roof of the Sheraton Universal Hotel, March, 1979. Photo credit: Warner Bros.

Whenever she makes a high jump, she makes sure everything is set up properly. Then she stands and concentrates. She blocks everything else out. She "thinks positive." The strong faith she has in God helps. She aims, jumps, and turns her mind off. Her blue-green eyes sparkle as she laughs and comments that she's happy when she lands.

Her *Wonder Woman* jump set a new record for women's high falls, but the people at the "Guinness Book of World Records" asked if she could make it even higher. On December 9, 1979, Kitty went to Devonshire Downs in Chatsworth, California to try. She would attempt to jump into an air bag from 175 feet.

This jump would be even more dangerous than the *Wonder Woman* jump. First, she would be jumping from 50 feet higher in the air. And second, she would be jumping from something moving, a helicopter. She had never done that before.

The morning started out cold. The sky was clear, and not even a hint of breeze touched the leaves on distant trees. That was good. If there was too much wind the jump would have to be called off. Kitty stood at one end of the huge field, wrapped in a blue ski jacket against the chill. Friends came, they chatted and wished her luck. She hugged them and smiled, happy to have them there, but each time a small crowd gathered she seemed to drift away to stand by herself.

The first practice jump was scheduled for 9:30 A.M. but things were running late. People scurried around making arrangements but Kitty stayed off by herself. She was not one to scurry. Besides, she trusted Dar Robinson and his team to work things out. Her job was to jump.

Kitty and stuntman Dar Robinson with his sons Shawn and Troy at Devonshire Downs, Chatsworth, California, just before her record-breaking jump.

By 10:00 Kitty was still waiting, still looking calm leaning against the helicopter that would take her up for her first practice jump. She gazed around the huge field where other people were attempting to break other records.

A paramedic came over from the ambulance parked nearby and introduced himself to her. "I'll be helping you if you need it," he said. "Is there anything I should know . . . any allergies to medications, anything?"

Kitty shook her head. "No," she said, "no allergies, I'm healthy."

"Well, good luck then," he said and left her alone again.

Then Dar came to talk with her. He is a stuntman too, and he holds the world free fall record. It was his air bag she'd be using and she'd be getting her cues when to jump from him. He's a good man to rely on. He set his own record jumping from a helicopter. He knows it takes practice to know when to jump from something moving and he's had a lot.

Kitty watched as he talked.

"My man back there," he pointed toward the south end of the field, "will signal the helicopter pilot into place. I'll stand at the north end of the bag so I can see when you're in position. I'll stand with my arms out. When I drop them you go. Right away. With the 'copter moving you won't fall straight down, you'll travel forward in the air before you land. You have to jump the instant I say or you could miss the bag."

"OK," she said, nodding. She understood.

The air bag that had been a giant pile of nylon a few minutes ago was blown up. It was a beautiful bright blue on top, shiny silver on the sides. Inflated it was 18 feet high and almost the size of a small house. Dar's crew checked it over carefully to make sure it was ready. Dar made a practice jump from 120 feet. Then it was Kitty's turn. She would make three practice jumps at 150 feet. They had to know that she was landing right before taking it up any higher.

As the helicopter circled for the first practice jump, another helicopter followed taking pictures. Kitty stood on the skids of the 'copter watching for Dar's signal below. She came closer, closer. Wait — the air bag blew down. The camera helicopter had come too close. The fierce wind made by its propellers made the bag collapse. Her helicopter came down and she waited while the bag was put up again.

At Devonshire Downs, Kitty does not seem at all concerned about her jump.

Then she was back up in the air. She stood on the skids and looked down. Her bright red sweater made her easy to spot even that far up in the air. The 'copter came closer to the air bag, closer. Kitty waved to the pilot, trying to get him to move. She moved back and forth along the skids trying to get where it looked good to jump. She had to go pretty soon, or else. Kitty sat down. It was a pass.

In front of the helicopter from which she will jump to set a new woman's free fall record. December, 1979.

The next time the helicopter came into position was a pass too. Finally the third try she got the signal. She leaned, then let go. She fell, and fell. Then she tucked a little and landed. Ten seconds later she crawled off the bag. She had twisted her knee a little when she landed but she didn't mention it. She was fine.

She and Dar had another conference.

"You waited a second too long, you have to go right when I signal."

Kitty frowned. "But it didn't look like I was in the right place."

"You were. Remember, with the 'copter moving, you're going to travel forward in the air. You're not just going to drop straight down."

"Can't the helicopter stop?"

"No, the down-wash from the propellers will blow the bag down."

Kitty nodded. OK, she'd try it again. Both agreed the next jump was better.

The falls that took seconds to make seemed to take forever to set up. It was already 12:30, lunchtime. Everyone took a break and everyone except Kitty ate. She sat, still looking calm, watching.

At 1:30 the bag was inflated again. Kitty did one more practice jump from 150 feet. Finally at 2:00 she was ready for the record jump. She climbed back into the helicopter for the last time.

The announcer called out over the loudspeaker that this was the record attempt. People stopped what they were doing and looked up, shading their eyes against the sun.

Up in the sky the helicopter looked like a toy. Kitty was small as a pencil lead as she stood waiting for the signal. The 'copter came closer . . . closer . . . there! She let go and fell forward and down toward the bag, down, down. She did it. From even higher than she had planned! She set a new women's free fall record, falling from what would be the eighteenth floor of a building — 180 feet.

Ready to go.

Kitty jumping to set a new world record.

She did it!

Chapter Seven

Kitty was kept very busy doing stunts and talking at deaf schools. But she wanted to do something else sometimes too.

With her love of speed and vibrating motors it was natural that she would be interested in Bill Frederick's new 48,000-horsepower hydrogen peroxide-powered rocket vehicle, the *Motivator*. Bill designed it to set a new world Land Speed Record (LSR). In 1965 Lee Breedlove had set the women's LSR at 308.56 mph. Kitty was sure she could go faster than that and it was arranged for her to try in the *Motivator*.

In September, 1976 she made her first test run in the 39-foot, three-wheeled "car" across El Mirage Dry Lake in Southern California. Her unofficial speed was 358 mph. That was faster than Lee. Now to make it official.

In October she went with a crew of friends and an official timer to Bonneville Salt Flats in Utah. When they got there they discovered the nine-mile course wasn't as smooth as they had thought it would be. What should they do? Go home without making a run? Try it and hope for the best? They were there and ready. Kitty was willing to go ahead and try. That's what they decided to do.

To make the record official, LSR rules say a person must make two runs in opposite directions, and within an hour of each other. That way, wind or slightly sloping ground that worked for the driver one way would work against him going in the other direction. The rule helps to balance things out. The average speed of the two runs is called the official speed.

Kitty had gotten new hearing aids that helped her hear some sounds but she couldn't hear the crew's countdown. How would she know when everyone was ready? The crew developed a series of cue cards so she could *watch* the countdown.

Kitty squeezed into the car and made a couple of runs, but every time she got going fast the car started weaving crazily from side to side. The car's aluminum wheels slipped and slid on the salt flats before she was anywhere near the speed she wanted to go, and she knew she couldn't handle it any faster. The try was called off. She was disappointed. Everyone else was disappointed too. There was nothing to do but pack everything up and go home. They would try again later somewhere else.

On December 4, on Oregon's dry Lake Alvord, Kitty pulled on her coveralls and helmet and once again climbed into the *Motivator*. Would everything work out all right this time, she wondered? When she climbed out of the car would she be the new record holder?

A mile-and-a-half ahead of the car's needle nose were the photocells that would time her run. Kitty fired the car up and flashed back and forth across the dry lake bed.

Her official speed was 322 mph. It was enough to break Lee's record. Kitty was the fastest woman on earth, but that wasn't enough. She wanted to set a record that would stand a long time. She wanted to go faster.

On December 6, 1976 she tried again. On the front of her white coveralls was pinned a tiny gold cross. She strapped herself in and aimed the *Motivator* back and forth across the dry lake bed again and again.

Run one, run two, run three. Every time she tried to go faster without losing control of the car. Her take-off's were so fast that each time 700 pounds of pressure pushed against her 100-pound body like a giant fist. It pushed against her chest. She couldn't breathe! She couldn't see very well, either. It felt as though she were going to pass out. The pressure was so great her skin slid back on her body, spreading tight against the front. Then she'd pass the photocells, the run was over. She'd coast to a stop and that part felt terrific, like she was in Heaven.

Photo taken just after Kitty set a new woman's land speed record. Photo Credit: Chuck Duncan.

Run four, five, six. Sometimes she'd go really fast in one run but the runs before and after would be slow. That brought down her average speed. She had to get two really fast runs in a row. . .

Run seven, eight. Eight was a slow one. Nine. There, nine was fast, really fast. If she could just do the next one that way. Everyone crossed their fingers and hoped. Run ten. It was fast! Everyone could feel it was. Was it fast enough? Kitty climbed out of the car, excited.

"How fast was that?" she asked. The official beamed as he told them the time. Wild whoops of happiness filled the air. People jumped up and down and hugged each other. She had done it! Her average speed topped Lee Breedlove's by over 200 mph. She had set a new record that was likely to stand for a long, long time. Kitty had set a new women's land speed record, racing across the desert at 512.710 mph.

In 1978 when someone suggested she try for another speed record she said OK, why not?

On July 25 she attempted to break the funny car speed record. A funny car looks like a regular car, only it's specially made of lightweight fiberglass and is fitted with a special engine. Kitty's funny car had the body of a Corvette.

The first run went smoothly, her time was good. The second run ended in disaster as she hit bumpy ground and the car hit a three-foot sand dune, bounced 200 feet through the air, then bounced end over end several times. The car was destroyed, pieces of it lay everywhere. Somehow Kitty was OK. She was also the new funny car speed record holder with an average time of 358 mph.

This is what was left of the funny car after the accident. Pieces were scattered everywhere.

She holds the speedboat speed record too, after racing a boat across Walker Lake in Nevada at an incredible 285.23 mph. She admits that was scary. There's nothing on the bottom of a boat to grab at the water and when she went fast it started weaving around. There was nothing she could do to control it. There weren't any brakes, of course, not even a parachute to slow her down. She just had to hang on and hope the boat wouldn't flip end over end. If it did, it would be pounded into splinters. She didn't like to think what would happen to her.

She made two runs, just enough to set the record and quit. She doesn't plan to do it again. Ever!

She does have a lot of other plans, though. Stunting has been good for her but it's long hours and hard, hard work. She plans to slow down soon. In an average month she flew to New York, Canada, Chicago and Ohio to do stunting jobs. That is a lot of time in airplanes. Other jobs may be closer to home but may still take hours to reach by car. That's too much traveling. It doesn't leave enough time for her to do some of the other things she'd like to do.

She misses having time to go off camping in the mountains. She misses playing football and basketball in the park. She'd like to have more time to spend with friends.

She hopes someday to find the right man to marry; she would like to settle down with him and adopt two deaf children of their own and, of course, she wants to open that school.

She plans to continue talking at schools to deaf children. She has a strong feeling about passing on the hope her parents gave her as a child.

She tells them she loves being deaf, and means it. It's so peaceful. It does cause problems sometimes, she says, but so do a lot of other things. Everybody has ups and downs, not just deaf people. She tells the children, if you have a problem, don't give up. Do something about it. Have faith in God. Have faith in yourself. Deafness, she tells them, is not a handicap but a challenge to conquer.

Kitty talks to children at Clark School for the Deaf in Northhampton, Massachusetts. June, 1979.

ABOUT THE AUTHOR

Karin Ireland says she has always had the urge to write and actually had 14 pen pals when she was in school. Four years ago she took a writing class and has been too busy to write letters ever since.

Ms. Ireland is involved in school and community affairs. She is an active swimmer, clogger, roller skater and horseback rider. Her other interests include travel, photography and the martial arts. She still claims to have plenty of time to write.

A native Californian, she still lives in that state with her husband and young daughter.